CAPE POETRY PAPERBACKS

TED WALKER

GLOVES TO THE HANGMAN

Ted Walker

GLOVES TO THE HANGMAN
POEMS 1969-72

JONATHAN CAPE
THIRTY BEDFORD SQUARE LONDON

FIRST PUBLISHED 1973
REISSUED IN THIS FORMAT 1975
© 1973 BY TED WALKER

JONATHAN CAPE LTD
30 BEDFORD SQUARE, LONDON WC1

ISBN 0 224 01096 4

Condition of Sale

*Printed and bound in Great Britain by
Richard Clay (The Chaucer Press) Ltd
Bungay, Suffolk*

Contents

Acknowledgments

The poems 'Boy by a river' and 'A celebration for autumn' (1970), 'After drought' and 'Snow in southern England' (1971), 'Letter to Barbados', 'August' and 'Afterwards' (1972) appeared originally in the *New Yorker* and were copyrighted © in the respective years shown by The New Yorker Magazine, Inc. Thanks are also due to: the *Poetry Review*, *Stand*, the B.B.C. Radio Three, *Workshop*, the *New York Times*, *Wave*, and the National Book League.

FOR MY BROTHER

O my gentle creatures

(after Salvatore Quasimodo)

O my gentle creatures, now
the green that was in the hills
turns ruinous with autumn.
Once more before nightfall we
shall hear the birds' last lament
and the call from the grey plain
rise toward the rumorous sea.
The scent of rain-wet wood, of
rabbit-burrows, here among
houses, among men, grows strong,
now, O my gentle creatures.

Slow eyes in this turning face,
this hand stretched toward heaven
where the ripping thunder is —
they belong to you, my wolves,
my blood-scorched foxes. All hands,
all faces, yours. And you tell
of futility, of life's
days worn as if by water
remorselessly away, while
in the garden children sing.
Far from us now, maybe? But
like shadows, less than shadows,
they slip to the air. This is
your voice. Yet perhaps I know
not everything has been.

A celebration for autumn

(for John Ormond)

Once more I welcome a purer darkness
Of evening in the hour of the year
Between summer and an end of summer,
When the soft air is songless as moss
Over the barn where the swallows are

Restless. Something has wearied the sun
To yellow the unmolested dust
On the bitter quince; something is lost
From its light, letting waxen bees drown
In their liquor of fatigue. But by last

Shadows of another season gone,
I live into beginning autumn
To see its silver, broken column
Of thready smoke ascending. Someone
Has gathered up his few leaves fallen

On the morning's webby lawn, who knows
Nothing of how I share them. I think
Of his hands at the live fire, and thank
Him in his private wood for what grows
Commonly for us toward the stars

I recognize of winter to come.
And I remember an August once,
With armfuls of slushing leaves, left since
Noon to dry by the hedge they fell from,
Shiny as the shears. Could we burn them

Now, I wheedled my grandfather, now?
Everything in its own due time,

He said, for fires need cold and autumn
Dark if you want their flowers to grow;
And who was I to call down the snow

Before its proper season? The weeks
Frittered on beyond the old man's dying,
And the ready pears, and my crying
In his garden-rows of empty sticks.
His fire shot higher than hollyhocks

One night when the smell of dead summer
Was too much to bear. It was for me,
Who had had hardly a breath easy
From the heavy hammer of asthma,
That frost assembled in that glimmer

Of thrown smoke, and prized into my blood
Like the feel of knives over the skin.
I lived on, into its cold. Again
I tread through a crisping grass; the hard
Air closes again, and I am glad.

Some troubled sleep it may take to bear
The slump of one less summer — but clean
The sun tomorrow, or the frail rain.
I shall breathe in refreshed September.
I have much to thank my autumns for.

Ancient winter

(after Salvatore Quasimodo)

Pallid come
your hands from
a pale fire
with desire
in a breath
of roses,
oakwood, death.

Now closes
old winter;
the birds go
from banter
into snow.
And like birds
and small sun,

so my words
will be gone
with the mist
among trees
and glories
of angels lost
in a dawn where

we are made air.

One magpie for sorrow

Now the rafters lift and shake
On blunt struts above the loft
And the flues whine down from the dark.
November again, month of my birth,
Blanches the stones bare to the earth

And gusts a single magpie, bereft
And cowering, to the stripped magnolia.
In my hearth the cold cinders shift
As I stare from the place where I belong.
Riffling another dying year, among

Dumb tokens of all I choose to be,
I pretend nothing can change. Yet,
As the day fades over the broken country
And this old white house prey to the weather,
I know my lie; know too well what other

Selves might enter. The magpie that
Cannot be hidden by darkness or by snow
Crouches under the wind. I shut out
Winter, whatever must come to pass.
Brittle twigs grint against the glass.

Snow in southern England

Not rare, or common, the snow
that visits our winters here:
a thin inch for every year
perhaps, and a foot or so
lost from the north one year in four;

and sometimes a stifled door
pushes back on a path of dead
sparrows grey as bits of bread,
broken to the dark before
some white moor fallen from the night.

But we live in a temperate
place, and never know true cold.
Brittling bones can grow old
in us, unsplintered by ice. Not
harder than my cruel summer doves

is the flocculence that lives
its day on the barren damson tree.
Warmed over by this January
sun, tomorrow the blush roofs
will show another season gone

of snow. I'd wish no more, more often,
than the falls we have, frequent as
sorrow. Or, brief as happiness,
want less, less often. The moon
risen this night is a white crow

roosting in a blizzard of stars.
The wind is stilled, and all I know
that I'd desire would be eyes
for dark beyond our buried places,
further off than this illumined snow.

New Forest ponies

They stopped from a gallop. Steam
left them like epiphanies
loose in the dusk. I saw them
whisking at snowflakes like flies.

It was a pair of forest
mares, briskets slung like hammocks
of fat matelots. With rapt lust
they browsed remnants of picnics

beside the Brockenhurst road.
Hobos, they rifled litter-bins,
turfing out chicken bones; then stood
casually among beer-cans,

posed for a snapshot album.
I nudged them along the verge
until their stallion came
prancing a disremembered rage

through the ice twilight. His strength
was flagged, a softening thong
of wash-leather. The cushy south
where he lives, where I belong,

would paddock him for gymkhanas,
currying his fourteen hands
to a genteel handsomeness.
Now he smelt like failing ponds,

shut cinemas. He began to come
at me. Gripping the fence-post,
I waited. But he ambled, a tame
elderly man in tweeds, lost

in some reverie of war,
all wildness shrunk. White of eyes
was mush, the shown teeth sulphur
dull. He let me feel him — thews,

veins, worn cordage to the touch.
I held him grass on my palm.
He cadged himself a sandwich;
mooched away, slavering jam.

Letter to Barbados

Dear far-off brother, Thank you for yours,
And for the gift you send of little shells.
Evening. It has been an April day
Like any you remember. I guess
How you miss the English spring, the way
A shower-cloud over a hillside spills

Between sunlight and sunlight, slowly.
Is it half a year since you've been gone?
While you gather up windfall nutmegs,
My white magnolia flowers fly
Withering from the twig like cotton rags
I must rake tomorrow from the lawn.

I wonder what news you want to hear:
That everything remains as it was
Before you left? That we are well? That
Swallows, like molecules of summer,
Warm on the wall behind the dovecote?
All is satisfactory in this house.

I read over again what you tell me.
Outside your window you've had grapefruits
Ripening through winter; there's a calf
You love to let suck your fingers. I
Relish these images of your new life,
Though the dinning sun above you hurts

My eyes as I gaze. Easier for you,
Perhaps, to think back to the shadow
Of this temperate, darkening garden,
Where I sit and look for my last few
Doves to come home. They will soon swoop down,
Just as you recall they always do,

From the roof; each full throat soon will soothe
Nightfall once more. This morning I made
A first cut of the grass since autumn.
It smelt sweet in the sun, in the swathe
Where I left it to dry. I fetched my gun
And sought out a sickly dove and killed

It clean, and let it warm where it fell.
Whether it is white, loosened feathers
I glimpse in the half-dusk or blossoms
Lifting with the wind I cannot tell,
But I am glad to have you share them.
There are words not used between brothers,

And you will understand if I send
No more than these, the shrivelling details
Of another lost and uneventful day.
The birds are folded now. I shall stand
A moment more in the dead grass we
Walked on. My palms close cold over shells.

The émigrés

Visiting from Britain, I take my ease
In a Massachusetts yard. Willows
Have opened overnight along the ridge;
This is the second spring I've seen this year.

I watch as my once-English hostess
Moves across the shadow of the spruces
At her door. She calls her home a cottage
And puts on homeliness like a sweater.

She's tried, over and over, to grow grass
Around the place; grass, and a few roses,
And even, look, a bit of privet hedge
To remind her of home in Warwickshire.

She brings me bourbon in an ice-packed glass
And tinkles on about the neighbours' houses.
Americanisms glint like a badge
Pinned onto her. She much prefers life here,

She protests, remembering what life was
For her in England — the dirt, rising prices,
Always having to live at the edge
Of her nerves. Not to mention the weather.

I stir my drink. 'I'd not mind it either,
For a while,' I say. Martins lodge,
Like my swallows at home, in crevices
Of her roof. 'Oh, purple martins, those

Damn things. I'll have to rake them down from there,'
She says. 'Mind you, it's not that I begrudge
Them somewhere to live. But if you saw the mess
They make, you wouldn't think me heartless.'

Now, in his office near a fall-out shelter
High over downtown Boston, husband Reg
Will be turning his calendar (English Views
In Summertime) into May. The two of us,

Last evening, swept the last of the winter
Cones into a heap. Outside his garage
Afterwards, he told me, watching the flames,
Of all his new, perpetual worries:

There's his job — they daren't have kids. And Russia.
And how he'll never keep up with the mortgage.
Not to mention the droughts, the six-foot snows,
In the yard where nothing English ever grows.

La más bella niña

(*after Luis de Góngora*)

The loveliest girl
of our home town,
the bride of a day,
is widowed and alone;
for the light of her eyes
to the war has gone,
and she tells her mother
who hears her mourn:

*O leave me, leave me
to weep by the sea.*

You told me, mother,
when I was young,
how pleasure is brief
but suffering long,
and, yes, you warned me
of him gone today,
who has taken the key
of my freedom away,

*O leave me, leave me
to weep by the sea.*

May these eyes that once
could see with delight
serve only for tears
and not for sweet sight;
they no longer have
a more fitting use,
for he's gone to the war
who was my peace.

O leave me, leave me
to weep by the sea.

Do not restrain me
or seek to find fault;
I deserve your lashes,
but don't rub salt.
If you wish me well,
don't treat me ill;
I'd be better off dead,
and silent, and still.

O leave me, leave me
to weep by the sea.

O my sweet mother,
who would not groan
though in her breast
beats a heart like stone;
who would not weep
as the years pass by
and the leaves of her youth
all wither and die?

O leave me, leave me
to weep by the sea.

The nights slip by
and the eyes have gone
that kept these lids
wide open till dawn;
gone; may they never
from loneliness stare
as mine from this bed
that has room to spare.

O leave me, leave me
to weep by the sea.

Polecats in Breconshire

Fine moths dropped from the darkness,
drifted like fallings of swarf
to dust the grasses whitely
where whitely flew the first scarf
of an owl as quiet as wool.

It was time for them to come
hot from a clammy chamber
under the summer mountain,
test the close air, and clamber
the foul chippings at their door.

They stood, rare as royalty,
in black and purplish fur
matted with the sweat of sleep;
relaxed as flaccid rubber,
they were ready to be stretched

the length of night's territory.
Seldom glimpsed by a human —
except, perhaps, at evening
by lonely widow-women
musty as old whinberries —

they loped for no enemy
they knew. Over the bracken
they leaped free; among the few,
too few to count, five of them ran
their bodies smooth in the dew.

And all the while there was night
they would shark through the thickets,

incising behind the skull
beasts that would be the pellets
of their pleasure. Armoured with

stench, and teeth to score tungsten,
they would slummock on fat eels.
On some road the good mother
would suckle her whelps. I would wonder
what they were, under my wheels.

At Pentre Ifan

Stolid endure the cromlechs
of Wales. For a thousand known
years before the Crucifix,
massive slabs with limbs of stone
presided over the hills

and are intact from passing
weathers of faith. Plain stillness
grips their tons: yet, like drinking
mammoths that flex their bodies
slowly to the water-hole,

they seem to tilt from the sky
when their blunt dusk shadows crawl
from under them. Ungainly
in the blatant day, they sprawl
unshapen as bales. You could

sleep beside them in the sun,
lifeless where the ancients lived,
for no ghost uses the noon.
But whoever has believed
something dwells beyond the skull,

once, belief upon belief
ago — strong in the simple
creed of dying into life —
must flinch when monumental
creatures of the antique dead

rise against the fading day.
Only some candid girl, led
cautious by her virgin boy,

might find here an easy bed.
They'd come to this holy place

from hollow lanes, at leaf-dark,
late sunlight sharper than glass
skimming off the sea to spike
among the holly. Nervous,
as though she were her own corpse,

he'd pass a hand over her,
lightly, as he'd feel these stones,
coming alone, years after.
From their cold he knows his bones
fingering beyond the last

innocence left him. Chastened,
he follows his shadow past
gorse flaming for night. Unpenned
sheep drop their cruds in the lost
grass. The gate grinds, unfastened.

Afterwards

Afterwards, we quarrel from love
And once again we are back
In our disparate bodies.
The room cools, almost darkness,

My fingers gripping the fallen quilt.
You lie as if at the edge of the sea,
The sun gone off the water.
Hair has the slipperiness of eelgrass.

Oh, the words you flung, I hear them,
Pebbles tumbling, smoothened with use;
But hurting; but individual; belonging
To us — worth keeping for themselves.

While you sleep, I gather them.
You shift. I listen for the city.
Tyre-hiss, a draining breakwater;
I remember finding a kittiwake, dead.

You are so cold. I should cover
This illicit skin awash in the moon.
I lift you as though you were mine
To keep. Let me see your eyes.

Villanelle

I would wish to die in some other place
Than where visitors come. I would be thrown
One morning of the winter on my face

In porous earth that would not leave the trace
Of where I lie. Not that I want it known
I would wish to die. In some other place,

Some other time, I might argue that case:
Waking, say, to a cancer and alone
One morning. Of the winter, on my face

I feel a flint wind blow, though clouds chase
May shadows. I dream the chalk hill whose bone
I would wish to die in. Some other place

Might serve as well for earth's final embrace;
And small matter where, so long as no one,
One morning of the winter, on my face

Touch the skull smile the soft rain will erase.
The morning finds my flesh as warm as stone.
I would wish to die in some other place.
One morning of the winter. On my face.

Boy by a river

Lymph, bled from a dead chalk,
and gauzes of watered milk
slubbered a certain turf
among dry hills, far off,
and lived, kindling his river.

But he was young — such inklings never
trickled into his bigger knowledge.
He brazened the estuary's edge
by a rusty wharf, and could stare
only to seaward. For there

where he lived it was a wide
sliding on the silent tide;
or, shrunk to its thews, sawed itself raw
across broken rock and the bare
ribs of picked ships. And all he knew

of meadow brooks that grew
pure between upland pasture —
of barley fields upriver
that spared through their flints thin
tributaries of cress hidden

from fish — he had learned from a friend
the fresh waters had lately drowned,
who had spoken of simple shallows
where the swimming was good. Those
reaches would flow through his mind

always; already their pools wound
a body round in an endless whirl
for his memory. In time, he would while

a summer's hour tracing the source,
and with his man's strong hand force

back for an instant the feeble
killer into dumb earth. It would dribble
in his tight fingers slowly,
then he would dry them. Now he let fly
his stones that the brimming ebb

accepted with a sip. In the crab
holes he supposed they would rest,
too deep, too heavy to move. The last
of the white and rolling bones might be
shifting somewhere near. This he

believed, though for years he'd refuse
all else he was told of the river. His
eyes fixed on the cormorant he knew,
he would be old before the blue
jewel of a kingfisher filled them

and he followed with the wind upstream
that lifted ripples into the flood.
There were lost otter runs, his friend had said,
and long golden mullet that laze
under the banks where wildfowl graze.

After drought

The river was its dregs —
Not water but stuck dags
Flung from the sun. One pool
Shrank to a cellar smell.

You could have picked trout
Like flowers. They had got
Wedged in lilies, each back
Stretched and dry as a stalk.

In the night I remembered
Them pressed tight to the lid
Of their element as
I grappled my jammed windows.

I had fire-damp on the lung.
The thought of gills pummelling
At brute gas had me sweat.
When first it thundered it

Fluttered like a failing
Heart. Puny lightning
Flared brief as match struck
In a gust. Fragments broke

From the brick air — bits
Of wind and stabbed, long spots
To the spread palm. I came
Outside toward the storm

And stand now bare to its axe.
It smashes black to the trunks
Of great trees. While I breathe
Deep from seething rain, wraith

Shadows fan across grass
Whiter than gravel. Rivers
Are rising to their reeds.
A poem swims from its words.

August

It was a slow
river that slid
wide through level
country of fen
and of soft-earth
celery fields,

making no sound
of water all
one afternoon
but flowing dark
as leafage swept
in a wet heap,

no wind to make
its rushes creak,
stem against stem,
or rain to fall
hissing on its
taut water-skin.

It was gallons
calm as a vat
someone has stirred
and left to work
in its own time
to clarify.

It licked itself
as quietly as
a cat its fur
and no skiff came
or wherry on
the turning curds.

And but for the
flying dabchick
that sheered from my
quietness I
might not have moved
my eyes away

from the river's
porcelain surface
something must smash,
or ever known
how near the sea
downstream would flash

for a moment
as the last sun
of August died
in a closing
gap of summer
mist, autumn mist.

In the Midi

I speak of a sheer country.
Trees grew straighter than men.
Of those pines I will not say

One word more, or of the bog,
Or of the deserted barns
Like starved cattle whose backs sag.

And of the small and cautious
Creatures that keep in them now —
Fox and salamander

Damned by a master long since
Gone — I would say nothing more,
Save that they and his curses

Lurk, and prowl, and shall endure.
He lived alone, by the axe.
When the shallow plough struck rock,

Spark-showers lit off the quartz
And laughed in his face. Nights
In autumn, nothing was left but lax

Muscles slumped along the shafts.
Apples used to fall like hours.
He would come home heavy to tears.

His hand would not hold the glass
Steady. He took trembling draughts
Of wine from some far-off place.

He died on a road, in old age.
The blades he honed are still bright.
He slaked no thirst. No rage.

Pig pig

In 1386, the tribunal of Falaise sentenced a sow to be
mangled and maimed in the head and forelegs, and then
to be hanged, for having torn the face and arms of a
child and thus caused its death ... As if to make the
travesty of justice complete, the sow was dressed in man's
clothes and executed on the public square near the city-
hall at an expense to the state of ten sous and ten deniers,
besides a pair of gloves to the hangman.

(E. P. Evans: *The Criminal
Prosecution & Capital Punishment of Animals*)

I

Hefty, she was, that beast.
Sunned herself in the crust
of cruds she had lain in.
She was blacker than sin.

She dabbled her great crotch
in swill. If you would scratch
her with a bit of stick
you'd picked out of the muck,

she would grin like a slut.
She slobbered on the gate
her wench's gratitude
for apples. She was lewd

for putrid meat; crunched rough
splinters from a slate trough;
had a go at iron. She
was a whore, couldn't be

satisfied. We served her
with an old, borrowed boar.
He had to be dragged back
like hot dung on a truck.

II

Pigs are things. In Falaise
we esteem our horses.
Being proud, noble men
we prefer to be known

for our stables, not for
sour sties we would rather
hide from the off-comer.
In that stinking summer

I left a lass to feed
my swine. I had to ride
to the fair with a string
of thoroughbreds. Yearling

colts I'm famous for — ask
any man if I'd risk
a good reputation
palming off a dud 'un.

Prices fetched high that year.
Due to some foreign war
even your knock-kneed geld-
ing weighed his worth in gold.

III

I sold, had a skinful
of the best brewer's ale,
then headed out of town
astride my stallion.

One of the lads it was
found me in the bushes.
He'd come from mucking-out
and, by God, he smelt it.

But he hadn't the reek
of horse-dung. On his cheek
was a filthy sow-smear,
wet with a big soft tear.

I got up and whipped him
for saying I should come
back quick. He found my purse
and whistled in my horse.

Again I larruped him,
the lout. Then he said something about his sister,
dead. I dawdled faster.

IV

The brat was on a board,
her bits. The sow had gnawed
her face from her ringlets.
I'd seen sows break piglets —

runts of their abundance —
and swallow them. What chance
could a soft-boned child have
with jaws a man can't move

once they clamp? Someone had
bound the stump arms with bed-
linen ripped into strips.
The feet, gaunt as stirrups,

were bare, the batwing skin
left untorn. I drank down
a stoup of cider while
they simmered camomile

to make the corpse smell sweet.
She'd not an ounce of fat
on her. I saw quite plain
something had to be done.

V

Not that it was my fault,
mind. Peasants worth their salt
know better than allow
kids inside with a sow.

When she'd done bawling I
fetched the mother to my
house. She stank in her rags,
that hag treading my rugs.

She meant bother. She could
not stop the stable-lad
from gabbing in the pub,
she said. I let her sob

when I offered money,
felt tender for her. She
had, after all, been a nice
bit of *jus primae noctis*.

I'd see to it, I said.
She clawed her tangled head.
I couldn't see how, yet
I said I'd see to it.

VI

In her sty sprawled my sow-
murderess. I heard low
grunts as she permitted
suck. In the sun she bled

gently from a bludgeon-
gash. She'd been given one
hard across her poor old neck
with a blunted mattock.

Her litter swarmed on her
like lice on a scalp. Where
blood was she let them lick.
A pair of nipples stuck

out spare, like pinnacles.
Stout iron manacles
bit deep in her trotters.
Troubled by flies she was.

She lay helpless as scum
in a dungeon. They'd come
and chained their prisoner.
I felt angry for her.

VII

Ugly-mouthed and quiet
the men-folk stood about,
grim with clubs. I saw they
wished an eye for an eye.

Moment upon moment
they stood about, silent.
Their dumbness spoke of death,
of a tooth for a tooth.

With meekness they behaved.
Not a one would have dared
to murmur a word or
walk to the pigsty door.

The sow moaned from her pain
like a cancered woman.
I told them to go home.
I'd see them right, I told them.

Sunlight slammed on the dung
between us. The men hung
bare heads. Their cowardice
fattened on my promise.

VIII

When they buried the kid,
I processed at the head
of the cortège. If I'd
not been at that graveside,

things might have turned bad. My
tribute was a lily-
wreath, the biggest of all.
The mother seem grateful.

It was I let the box
nice and slow to the six-
foot hole, was I let drop
a clod onto the cheap

wood lid. Then it was I
that led them solemnly
by the chain of their grief
to my welcoming roof.

I that threw wide the door.
I that spoke of the Law.
I that called upon God
to exact blood for blood.

IX

I found a precedent:
a bullock had been sent
mangled to the scaffold
for murdering a child.

Unravelling the Latin,
I knew it could be done:
the family would attest
and I'd see to the rest.

I hired the village thug
to guard the convict pig.
He fed her bread, not swill.
The parish got the bill.

I called in Maître Jehan,
my boozing companion,
to prosecute. Some sense-
less lush got the defence.

We booked the city hall
for the day of the trial.
Judge Rouge, swigging my wine,
appointed me hangman.

X

With all due reverence
the oafs gave evidence
on the day. In the dock
my sow slithered in muck.

Once she managed to drag
her bulk up like a lag
and lean over. Laugh!
It was farce, right enough.

But we played it serious:
only let po-faces
slacken for Rouge's jokes.
We wanted no mistakes

at this stage of the game.
The court-room was a slum
of roughs turning ugly
looks on the likes of me.

Jehan pitched it good and strong
though, and nothing went wrong.
The sow was found guilty
of eating flesh on a Friday.

XI

Mangle and hang the sow,
old Rouge said: Do it now.
I was aproned, masked and gloved.
This was the bit I loved.

God, it was Hell's delight.
I got that chained-up brute
again and again in
the limbs. Cracking the spine

was like splitting a flint
with a grubber. I bent
a great crowbar on her,
smashing her to rubber,

let the wet brain slop out
like spawn in a bucket.
Slut, I was thinking, slut,
by Christ don't you love it.

What really pricked me on
was having that whoreson
rabble agog as I
did that thing in a sty.

XII

After I'd had enough,
somehow they prized me off
her cadaver. They dressed
it up, at my request,

in clothes I provided:
shirt and breeches of red
velveteen, my best grey
bonnet of soft corduroy.

They sat it on a cart
with me up beside it.
Garlanded, we were hauled
in style to the scaffold.

We had to take a winch
to that heap of a wench;
with ropes round her armpits
we raised her hundredweights.

She dripped like a vast bag
of fruit on a licking dog.
The mob cheered. I could see
they pretended she was me.

XIII

The carcass (hangman's perks)
was mine. I cut some hunks
of offal for the kites,
butchered the rest as joints

for salting down. I ate
well all that winter. It
had been a good day's work
when that sow became pork.

We had some fun. I got
some good gloves out of it.
It was the parish paid
the profits my cronies made.

Even the peasants did
well — one less mouth to feed.
And my fame got around.
In all France you'll not find

a richer ranch than mine.
I can die a happy man,
knowing how justice was seen
through me to have been done.

Letter to Marcel Proust

I

Monsieur, when I first met you (introduced
    by a Cambridge don eighteen years ago)
there wasn't much about you I cared for.
    Semites I loathed, and next to Semites, queers;
never having fancied fellers, I fought off
    two-pound notes with roustabout righteousness,
and duffed up a bent yid once with a wire brush.
    What's more, my father being a working bloke
who'd been on the dole through my 'thirties boyhood,
    I'd learned by heart to put grub before ethics,
so that the world of Albertine and Madame Verdurin
    unfolding between your punctilious semi-colons
wasn't, so to speak, du côté de chez moi.
    To one of my generation of yobbos
who had inherited the posher universities,
    all that palaver in scented drawing-rooms
was dated as Zeppelins, a right load of shite.
    We turned every snobbery upside-down
and parodied a life we never would live:
    (not for us the tea-time punt to Grantchester
but sooner a canoe to a pub in Trumpington).
    But, Thanks, mate, I told my broken supervisor,
bidding him tara with a wave of the ration-book
    that marked the page we'd got to in *Swann*.
One day you'll remember all this, he said,
    moithering off towards the Combination Room,
à la recherche du ton perdu.

II

Today, bombing southwards on Autoroute 6
    à mi-chemin between Paris and Lyon,
one of my bus-load of dumb Yankee students
    offered me a madeleine from a plastic bag.
Ever the pedagogue, I seized the opportunity
    to give my spiel (lasting 40 kilometres)
on the involuntary memory, monsieur, and you.
    Christ, what a drag — like, man, who needs it?
was what I got from the weirdo freak.
    (Though later, at the zinc in the comfort-station
I smiled to observe that the woolly number
    was dunkin' a thoughtful Donut in a demi-tasse.)
Oh, the immutable ghastliness of students!
    Marcel (est-il permis?), I too am nostalgic
for the decencies of life I see in decay:
    I want no part of the acid-head commune
sharing out equally its bread and its crabs
    (any more than I'd want the return of privilege
and the tittling *Tatler* and its snaps of debs);
    yet maybe we're wrong to despair of the future,
its perspective of instant beds stretching end to end.
    There will always be those to share our snobbery
for what comes difficult, like Art and Love,
    and even (dare one mention it?) tolerance
by which, since Israel and the Wolfenden Report,
    hetero queer-bashing fascists like me
have learned, with time, to be friends with such as you.

Sundays

(after Jules Laforgue)

How aimless, passionless, the rain is, lover,
Raining endlessly into the river ...

The river sleeps in its Sunday serge;
Upstream, downstream, not one barge.

Evensong is pealing over the town,
Along the riverbank no couples are seen.

A girls' school passes (poor little loves!)
Several already with winter gloves.

Here's one with neither gloves nor coat,
Dressed all in grey, a sorry sight.

She's broken ranks — she's a fair runner!
But O, my God, what *has* got into her?

Head-first she's flinging herself into the water,
No boatman or Alsatian to get her.

The lights go on; how late it's getting:
Think of the town, its cosy setting.

The rain keeps raining, dampening the river,
Aimlessly, with no passion whatsoever.

Pierrots

(after Jules Laforgue)

On a starched strawberry a neck
likewise stiff; from this will stick
a cold-cream face with the look
of a wet-brained thick.

Eyes awash with opium
swim in vice's aquarium,
the clownish mouth's operculum
charmed as a strange geranium.

A lidless manhole mouth, a yawn
wide as a crevasse sags open,
vapid the smile, distant, thin
as the Giaconda grin.

Flour-white caps are rammed on those
black silk bands that bind their brows;
from crow's feet their laughter grows,
an ace of clubs each puckered nose.

They wear, for lack of precious stone,
a scarab brooch like an Egyptian;
plucked from a vacant lot, the dandelion
buttonhole suits them fine.

They go their way, living upon
fresh air, vegetables now and then,
rice whiter than their costume, an
eight-minute egg, a mandarine.

Members of the Sect of the Lily,
having no truck with God, they gaily
chant that everything will be
right as rain come Mothering Sunday.